13 Colonies

Connecticut

13 Colonies

CONNECTICUT

The History of Connecticut Colony, 1633–1776

Roberta Wiener and James R. Arnold

Raintree
Chicago, Illinois

© 2005 Raintree
Published by Raintree,
A division of Reed Elsevier, Inc.
Chicago, IL

All rights reserved. No part of this publication may be reproduced or transmitted in any form or by any means, electronic or mechanical, including photography, recording, taping, or any information storage and retrieval system, without permission in writing from the publishers.

For information, address the publisher:
Raintree, 100 N. LaSalle, Suite 1200, Chicago, IL 60602

Printed in China by South China Printing.
09 08 07 06 05
10 9 8 7 6 5 4 3 2 1

Library of Congress Cataloging-in-Publication Data
Cataloging-in-publication data is on file with the Library of Congress.

Every effort has been made to contact copyright holders of any material reproduced in this book. Any omissions will be rectified in subsequent printings if notice is given to the publishers.

Disclaimer
All the Internet addresses (URLs) given in this book were valid at the time of going to press. However, due to the dynamic nature of the Internet, some addresses may have changed, or sites may have changed or ceased to exist since publication. While the author and publishers regret any inconvenience this may cause readers, no responsibility for any such changes can be accepted by either the author or the publishers.

The paper used to print this book comes from sustainable resources.

Some words are shown in bold, **like this.** You can find out what they mean by looking in the glossary.

Title page: A view of Middletown, which grew to be a busy port in the 1700s

Opposite: Connecticut's farms spread out from the towns into the fertile areas beyond them.

The authors wish to thank Walter Kossmann, whose knowledge, patience, and ability to ask all the right questions have made this a better series.

PICTURE ACKNOWLEDGMENTS

COURTESY AMERICAN ANTIQUARIAN SOCIETY: 14, 27 bottom, 33, 38 bottom ARCHITECT OF THE CAPITOL: 8, 13, 52, 56 WILLIAM CULLEN BRYANT, ET. AL., *Scribner's Popular History of the United States*, 1896: 10, 15, 23 bottom COLONIAL WILLIAMSBURG FOUNDATION: Cover, 5, 6, 17, 27 top, 31-32, 32 bottom, 39, 45 CONNECTICUT HISTORICAL SOCIETY, HARTFORD: Title page, 20, 21, 28-29, 32 top, 38 top, 53, 54 top, 57 JOHN W. DEFOREST, *History of the Indians of Connecticut*, 1851: 24, 35, 44 J.G. HECK, *Iconographic Encyclopedia of Science, Literature, and Art*, 1851: 7 ERIC INGLEFIELD: 59 LIBRARY OF CONGRESS: 9, 18 right, 19, 23 top, 25, 34, 36, 43, 48, 49, 50-51, 54 bottom, 55 MILITARY ARCHIVE & RESEARCH SERVICES, ENGLAND: 47 NATIONAL ARCHIVES: 31, 46, 58 COURTESY OF THE NATIONAL GUARD BUREAU; "First Muster," a National Guard Heritage painting, copyright Don Troiani, 1985: 22 NATIONAL PORTRAIT GALLERY, LONDON, ENGLAND: 12 U.S. NAVAL ACADEMY MUSEUM, ANNAPOLIS: 41 I.N. PHELPS STOKES COLLECTION, NEW YORK PUBLIC LIBRARY: 11, 42-43 SOUTH CAROLINA HISTORICAL SOCIETY: 18 left

CONTENTS

PROLOGUE: THE WORLD IN 1633		6
1.	NEW ENGLISH BEGINNINGS	13
2.	CONNECTICUT IN 1633	16
3.	THE ENGLISH TIDE	19
4.	MAKING A LIVING IN CONNECTICUT	28
5.	NEW ENGLAND BATTLES	34
6.	THE ROAD TO INDEPENDENCE	45
EPILOGUE		57
DATELINE		60
GLOSSARY		61
FURTHER READING		62
WEBSITES		63
BIBLIOGRAPHY		63
INDEX		64

Connecticut

Prologue: The World in 1633

In the year 1633, Massachusetts Puritans began expanding into present-day Connecticut. By this time, more than 4,000 English people had begun new lives in Virginia, Massachusetts, and New Hampshire. Some 500 **Dutch** colonists had settled in New Netherland, the name they gave their possession in present-day New York.

Europe had begun to explore the wider world during the Renaissance, a 150-year period of invention and discovery beginning during the 1400s. Advances in navigation and the building of better sailing ships allowed longer voyages. So began the Age of Exploration, with great seamen from Portugal, Spain, Italy, the Netherlands, France, and England sailing into uncharted waters. The explorers reached Africa, India, the Pacific Ocean, China, Japan, and Australia. They encountered kingdoms and civilizations that had existed for centuries.

A European mapmaker's view of the world around 1570

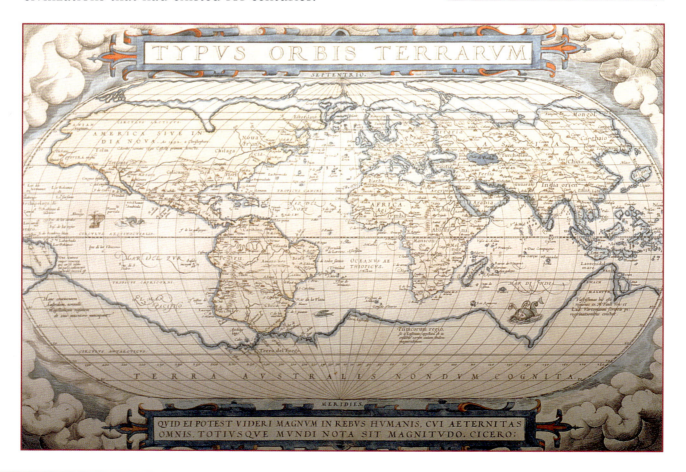

6

Prologue: The World in 1633

The Great Wall of China, about 4,000 miles (6,437 kilometers) long and an average of 30 feet (9 meters) high, was built around 200 B.C.E. and rebuilt during the 1400s and 1500s to defend China from northern tribes.

   Europeans did not yet have a clear idea where all these lands lay. But the Portuguese and other Europeans knew enough to see great opportunities. They saw the chance to grow rich from trade in exotic spices. They saw people they wanted to convert to Christianity. They saw the chance to make conquests of their own and expand their countries into great empires. And not least, they saw the dark-skinned people of Africa and, thinking them a different species, they saw the chance to capture and sell slaves. Traders from the Netherlands began joining other Europeans in voyaging to Africa, Asia, and the Pacific to trade in spices and slaves. They eventually formed the Dutch East India Company, which would one day gain a foothold in Connecticut.
   The voyages from Europe to these distant shores went around Africa. This made the trip long and dangerous. So,

Connecticut

Many artists have imagined and made pictures of Columbus coming ashore on the far side of the Atlantic.

European explorers began to sail westward in search of shortcuts. In 1492, the explorer Christopher Columbus landed on an island on the far side of the Atlantic Ocean and claimed it for Spain. He thought that he had actually sailed all the way around the world and come to an island near India. Years of exploration by numerous sailors passed before the people of Europe realized that Columbus had been the first European of their era to set foot in a land unknown to them. They called this land the New World, although it was not new to the people who lived there. After Columbus, Amerigo Vespucci claimed to have reached the New World. Whether he actually did or not, in

Prologue: The World in 1633

Giovanni da Verrazano was the first European known to have explored the east coast of the present-day United States.

> AMERICA: LAND THAT CONTAINS THE CONTINENTS OF NORTH AMERICA AND SOUTH AMERICA

1507 a mapmaker put his name on a map, and the New World became **America**, or the Americas. Still looking for a shortcut to the riches of Asia, European explorers continued to sail to North and South America. They began to claim large pieces of these lands for their own nations.

The first English ship to cross the Atlantic Ocean was commanded by the Italian-born John Cabot in 1497. Cabot's exploration of the eastern coast of Canada formed the basis for all of England's future claims to North American colonies.

A series of explorers journeyed to the eastern coast of North America, and several of them explored the coast of New England, including Connecticut. The Italian seaman Giovanni da Verrazano commanded a French expedition in 1524 and explored and charted the coast from the

Connecticut

Walter Raleigh sent colonists to America in 1587, and they were set ashore on Roanoke Island, in present-day North Carolina. When English ships returned to Roanoke in 1590, they found only a one-word message and a deserted settlement.

SASSAFRAS: TYPE OF TREE WHOSE BARK WAS USED FOR FLAVORING OR MEDICINAL PURPOSES

Carolinas to Maine. The little-known Esteban Gomez charted a portion of the New England coast for Spain the following year.

In the meantime, Walter Raleigh sponsored expeditions to America and claimed for England a large area of land he called Virginia. The disappearance of his colonists from Roanoke Island some time after 1587 remains an enduring mystery.

In 1603 English trader Martin Pring sailed to New England in search of **sassafras** and other trade goods. French explorer Samuel de Champlain then spent two years charting the New England coast and searching out a site for a French settlement, but hard winters and French politics combined to defeat the effort.

Members of the Virginia Company, which had founded the colony at Jamestown, at the same time sponsored a New England colony on the coast of Maine. This colony failed because, after one winter, the settlers found life too harsh. The unsuccessful colonists returned to England in 1608.

Prologue: The World in 1633

Not to be outdone by the exploring sea captains of their rivals, the Netherlands joined the search for a passage to Asia. In 1614, Dutch explorer Adriaen Block sailed up the Connecticut River as far as Windsor, the eventual site of the first English settlement.

Former Virginia colonist Captain John Smith explored and mapped the coast of New England in 1614, and his description kept interest in the area alive. But New England, with its cold northern winters, needed settlers with a special kind of endurance to found a lasting colony. The devoutly religious **Pilgrims** and **Puritans** were the first to have such endurance.

Religious conflict had occurred often in Europe. This caused English Christians to begin looking for a religious

Captain John Smith returned from Jamestown, Virginia, to England, and then sailed again across the Atlantic to explore and map the New England coast. His book, *A Description of New England*, painted a rosy picture. Smith called it a "paradise."

11

Connecticut

haven in America. For centuries in western Europe, Christianity and Roman Catholicism had been one and the same, with all Christians ruled from Rome by the Pope. But in 1517, Martin Luther, a German monk, protested some of the actions of the Roman Catholic Church. This began the **Protestant** Reformation. In 1534, the English King Henry VIII took advantage of the Protestant Reformation. The Pope would not grant him a divorce, so he broke from the Catholic Church, formed the Church of England, and declared himself its head. The Church of England, also called the **Anglican** church, became a Protestant church, independent of the Pope, but still Christian.

Queen Mary restored Catholicism as the official religion of England in 1554. She executed more than 250 people who had continued practicing Protestantism. For this reason, people called her "Bloody Mary." Five years later, Queen Elizabeth I restored the Church of England. Under her rule, and that of the next two kings, Catholicism was outlawed, and those who practiced it faced arrest. Even under Protestant rule, however, many English Protestants grew dissatisfied with the Church of England. Among them were the Pilgrims and the Puritans.

For most people, life in England in the early 1600s was hard. The Stuart **dynasty** had followed the great Queen Elizabeth I to the throne. Whereas Elizabeth had been tolerant, the Stuarts seemed to many to act like tyrants. Rich people had taken over much of the rural land, forcing poor people to leave the countryside and move to urban centers to search for jobs. During the first half of the century London grew by more than fifty percent. Crowded conditions caused disease epidemics, including the terrible bubonic plague, to be more deadly. In 1618 the Thirty Years War began, and this, too, caused great suffering and loss of life and property. England joined with other Protestant nations to fight Catholic powers in Spain and central Europe. Troubled people looked toward God and religion for help in such violent times. But religion, too, was a source of conflict.

Queen Elizabeth I was the daughter of King Henry VIII and his second wife Anne Boleyn. She did not marry and have children, so on her death the throne passed to her distant cousin, James I.

ANGLICAN: CHURCH OF ENGLAND, A PROTESTANT CHURCH AND THE STATE CHURCH OF ENGLAND

I.
NEW ENGLISH BEGINNINGS

Men and women who called themselves Puritans complained about the Church of England. They believed that it included too many sinners. The Puritans wanted to purify the church by expelling sinners. The Puritans also complained about many other aspects of the Anglican church. The Puritans wanted individual churches to have the power to control their own membership, and the members, in turn, to be able to control their local leaders. In this way the Puritan church would consist only of true believers. Puritans wanted to reform the church from within. Most English Puritans thought that the best way to accomplish their goals was to gain control of the government. They knew this would take time. Meanwhile, they believed that it was their Christian duty to support the church while they worked to reform it.

A much smaller group of Puritans had a different idea. They were unwilling to wait for political change. They wanted to separate themselves immediately from the corrupt and the sinners. The Anglican church responded by harassing and sometimes even killing those who promoted this idea of separation, so some of these small separatist groups fled to the Netherlands. Among them was a group that became known as the Pilgrims. In 1608 the Pilgrims emigrated to

The Pilgrims praying before departing the port of Leyden, the Netherlands

Connecticut

The Dutch claimed that their colony of New Netherland included all of Connecticut. In 1647, the Dutch governor, Peter Stuyvesant, wrote to the English governor of New Haven colony and addressed the letter to New Haven, New Netherland. The English governor refused to answer.

Amsterdam. Later they moved to the port of Leyden. In 1620, about 75 Pilgrims took the bold step of crossing the Atlantic Ocean to settle in America, where they founded Plymouth Colony on the coast of Massachusetts.

In the years after the founding of Plymouth Colony, new English settlements sprang up in Massachusetts. Some proved failures and were abandoned while others prospered and grew.

In 1630, John Winthrop and about 1,000 Puritans came to Massachusetts to settle around Boston Bay. They came with their own **charter** and called their new land the Massachusetts Bay Colony. Unlike the Pilgrims, Winthrop's colonists had financial backing and came with ample supplies. They quickly occupied the best sites and set to work planting crops.

New English Beginnings

Meanwhile, the Dutch, having founded the colony of New Netherland, extended their colony's border northward by establishing a trading post, Fort Good Hope, near present-day Hartford, Connecticut, in 1631. They purchased land, furs, lumber, and food from the native peoples in exchange for guns, tools, cloth, and alcoholic drink.

The Massachusetts Bay Colony grew rapidly. Soon 2,000 immigrants were coming to the colony each year and most of them were Puritans. The newcomers settled all along the Atlantic coast from Maine—which at this time was part of Massachusetts—to Long Island, off the coast of present day New York and Connecticut. They also spread inland up the major rivers to found new towns as far west as Springfield, Massachusetts. The entire region came to be called New England. The English ignored Dutch claims to Connecticut and explored along the Connecticut River. Edward Winslow of Plymouth was the first Puritan to explore the Connecticut River Valley in 1632. In 1633, a group of settlers from Plymouth bought riverside land from the **Native Americans** and founded a settlement that later became the town of Windsor.

> **NATIVE AMERICANS:** PEOPLE WHO HAD BEEN LIVING IN AMERICA FOR THOUSANDS OF YEARS AT THE TIME THAT THE FIRST EUROPEANS ARRIVED

The Dutch finally surrendered Fort Good Hope and their other Connecticut forts to the English in 1653, after the Connecticut militia marched on Long Island and tried to claim it. The English wasted no time in tearing down symbols of Dutch authority.

Connecticut

2.
Connecticut in 1633

Connecticut is bordered by New York, Rhode Island, and Massachusetts, with a coast on the Long Island Sound, an inlet of the Atlantic Ocean. It is considered the southernmost part of New England. The coastal lowland is a narrow strip of land along the coast. Connecticut's coast is rocky in some areas and lined with sandy beaches in others. Inland from the coastal lowland are the hilly eastern and western uplands. Between the two upland regions lies the central lowland, which has good farm land. The highest point in the state is Mount Frissell, at 2,380 feet (725 meters), in the northwestern corner of Connecticut.

The Connecticut River runs through the central lowland and part of the eastern upland, before draining into the Long Island Sound. The Native Americans called the river Quinnehtukqut, meaning "beside the long tidal river." The Housatonic, Naugatuck, and Thames rivers also flow southward through Connecticut and into Long

> **Algonquians:** Native Americans who speak one of several related languages belonging to the Algonquian family of languages; Algonquian speakers once lived over an area extending from New England to the Carolinas, as well as in parts of Canada and around the Great Lakes

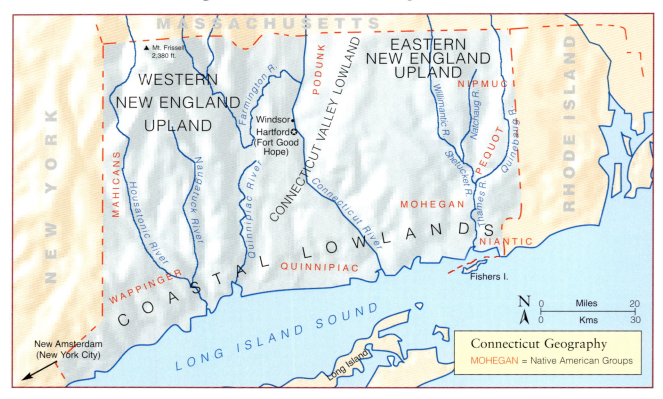

16

Connecticut in 1633

Island Sound. Connecticut has more than 1,000 lakes, many formed by glaciers. Connecticut has colder temperatures in the upland regions, but the central lowlands of the Connecticut River Valley are warm enough to grow tobacco.

Native Americans began arriving in New England around 10,000 years ago. By the time Europeans began exploring New England, more than 5,000 **Algonquian-**speaking Native Americans belonging to about 16 tribes lived in the area that became Connecticut.

The most powerful Native Americans were called the Pequots. They moved into the area during the late 1500s, occupying land that had belonged to other native peoples. By the year 1600, at least 2,000 Pequots lived along the coast and the border with Rhode Island. Other native peoples feared them and called them "destroyers."

The other major tribe in Connecticut was the Mohegan, whose name means "wolf." They were Algonquian speakers and were not the same people as the Mahicans of New York. At first the Mohegans lived in the Thames River valley. Later they expanded their territory to the north and west. By 1600, about 2,200 Mohegans lived in Connecticut.

Small bands of Mahicans lived along part of the border with New York. Niantics lived on the coast from Niantic Bay to the Connecticut River. The coast and the river valleys were home to a number of smaller groups, including the Wappinger, Quinnipiac, and Podunk peoples. Small groups of Nipmucs lived in northeastern Connecticut.

The native peoples of the region lived in wigwams, built by covering a framework of poles with bark and animal skins. They survived by hunting and fishing, gathering wild plants, and growing corn, squash, and beans. They also grew tobacco for ceremonies.

At the time the first Europeans arrived, Connecticut was almost entirely wooded, with only a small area of coastal marshes and fields cleared by Native Americans. Deer, bear, and wolves lived there, along with smaller animals such as foxes, porcupines, raccoons, and beavers.

Native Americans grew tobacco as far north as the Connecticut River valley, and English people came to like tobacco enough to grow it themselves. A New England Puritan woman wrote, " I remember with shame, how, formerly, when I had taken two or three pipes, I was ready for another, such a bewitching thing it is; but I thank God he has now given me power over it; surely there are many who may be better employed than to lie sucking a stinking tobacco pipe."

Connecticut

Right: An Algonquian village. The women tended the fields, which the men had cleared. They usually managed to grow or find just enough food to survive. If they had any extra food, the men set out in canoes to trade with other tribes.

Below: The English were intrigued by reports that beavers cut down trees and changed the landscape. This drawing, called "The Industry of Beavers," was published in 1715.

Corn, Squash, and Beans

Clearing land to create open fields for planting took a lot of hard work. Before Europeans arrived, the native peoples of eastern North America did not have metal tools such as saws and axes. They cleared land with stone tools and used controlled fires. Fields cleared with such difficulty had to be used efficiently. The Native Americans worked out a system of growing three crops at a time, so that each crop benefited the others.

First they planted corn in small mounds three or four feet apart, using fish as fertilizer. When the corn stalks had grown a couple of feet tall, squash, pumpkin, and bean seeds were planted around them. The corn stalks provided support for the climbing bean vines and shade for the squash vines that ran along the ground. The squash vines helped reduce weeds and slowed evaporation of moisture from the soil. Bean plants took nutrients from the air and added them to the soil (called nitrogen fixing). The three-crop system was a neat solution to a difficult challenge.

3.
THE ENGLISH TIDE

Under Governor Winthrop's leadership, the Puritans of Massachusetts had organized an efficient government that included courts, police, and tax collectors. The Puritans believed that only devout churchgoers were suitable for leadership positions in their colony. They discriminated against nonbelievers. Puritan control of the Massachusetts Bay Colony extended into many aspects of life. Their goal was to create a stable Christian society that remained true to Puritan ideals. Winthrop believed that people should live close together, not only for defense, but so they could guide one another in living according to Puritan laws.

However, the growing population of Massachusetts Bay was beginning to run out of land. People had heard of the fine farm land in the Connecticut River valley and sought permission to settle there. Winthrop was at first reluctant to let people move so far from the heart of his colony. However, the people needed more land, and permission was granted, provided the new settlements remained under the Massachusetts government.

The signing of the Mayflower Compact in 1620 by the men of Plymouth Colony. The Mayflower Compact established the idea that government depends on the consent of the people it governs. English settlers brought this idea with them to Connecticut.

Connecticut

English colonists built Hartford on land that once looked like this. The native peoples regularly set fires to clear out underbrush. When the first Europeans came to New England, they noticed that the forests were often so open that they looked like parkland.

The town of Wethersfield was founded in 1634 and settled by people from Watertown, Massachusetts. The first houses were built by the trader John Oldham and his associates.

In the summer of 1635, a group of English settlers moved from Dorchester to Windsor, occupying land purchased by the earlier settlers from Plymouth. A few months later another group of settlers moved to a site across the Hartford River from the Dutch fort, founding what later became Hartford. A hard winter drove some of these Connecticut settlers back to Massachusetts, but they returned in the spring.

In May 1636, Reverend Thomas Hooker of Newtown (Cambridge today), Massachusetts, led his congregation to build a new settlement at Hartford. The land around Newtown was rocky and difficult to farm, so they were tempted by reports of lush riverside meadows. However,

The English Tide

Thomas Hooker leading his congregation to Connecticut. Hooker was born in England in 1586 and educated at Cambridge. After becoming a Puritan minister, he left England for the Netherlands, and then came to Massachusetts in 1633.

Hooker and his congregation also had religious and political differences with the Massachusetts government. Hooker wanted to make it easier for people to become church members. He also believed that the clergy had too much influence over the government and argued that government authority belonged to the people. By people, however, he meant Puritans. Hooker's congregation received permission from the Massachusetts authorities to relocate. They trekked overland driving their cattle before them.

The following year, Hartford, Windsor, and Wethersfield joined together and elected a local government. This government had the power to act on local matters rather than wait for word from distant

Connecticut

> **MILITIA:** GROUP OF CITIZENS NOT NORMALLY PART OF THE ARMY WHO JOIN TOGETHER TO DEFEND THEIR LAND IN AN EMERGENCY
>
> **SACHEM:** ALGONQUIAN WORD FOR CHIEF

An early colonial militia

Massachusetts. It made laws relating to such matters as the control of stray hogs and the arming and training of **militia**.

The Pequot War

In selling land to the colonists, the Native Americans believed that they would continue being able to hunt and fish on land that was not planted with crops. Meanwhile, English settlers trespassed on land still owned by the Native Americans. Simmering resentments boiled over into murder. English traders killed a **sachem**, and in revenge Native Americans killed several English traders, including John Oldham, in 1636.

The English Tide

Soon after the burning of the Pequot village, Captain John Underhill published this orderly diagram of the attack.

No matter who may have begun these murderous exchanges, the killings gave the English an excuse to go to war against the Pequots, who stood in the way of their expansion. The English demanded that the Pequots pay a large fine and turn over the suspects along with several children as hostages. The Pequots refused, and an English war party from Massachusetts raided and looted Pequot villages. The Pequots then attacked the English fort at Saybrook and settlers at Wethersfield. At Wethersfield in April 1637 they killed nine English men and captured two women.

In May 1637, Connecticut—joined by Massachusetts Bay and Plymouth colonies, along with the Narragansetts and the Mohegans—planned its revenge for the attack on Saybrook. Captain John Mason and Captain John Underhill led English troops in a surprise predawn attack against the main Pequot village. They set the sleeping village on fire, surrounded it, and then killed everyone who tried to flee from the flames. No one knows for certain, but probably more than 400 Pequot men, women, and

A closer view of fire and slaughter

23

Connecticut

Early Connecticut

children died in just 30 minutes.

The Narragansetts, who hated the Pequots, were so horrified by the slaughter that they protested. Puritans in England protested as well when they heard of the attack. However, the New England Puritans believed that they had God on their side. Captain Underhill answered the protests, "We had sufficient light from the Word of God for our Proceedings."

The English force then cornered a group of Pequots in a swamp, killed all the men, and sold the women and children into slavery. The English were now free to occupy the Pequot lands. The Puritan religion taught that slavery was wrong except in the case of a captive taken in a just war. The colony's first slaves were captives taken in the Pequot War.

The war ended disastrously for the Pequots. Half of them had been killed, and the rest were sold as slaves or became subjects of rival tribes. The Mohegans,

The last of the Pequots were cornered and slaughtered in a swamp.

Narragansetts, and Niantics treated them very harshly. However, the remaining Native Americans had learned that they had no choice but to submit to all English demands if they wanted to avoid the same fate.

A Connecticut Constitution

The Massachusetts government divided up Connecticut land among the different groups of Puritan settlers. John Winthrop, Jr., son of the Massachusetts Bay governor, was appointed as temporary governor, with eight appointed advisers. Delegates from the three main towns of Hartford, Windsor, and Wethersfield then met to draw up a governing document for Connecticut. Early in 1639, they agreed on a document called the Fundamental Orders. This was the first written document to establish government by the consent of the people.

Approved male members of Puritan congregations were to elect the governor and his advisers. Full church membership was not granted to all Puritans, so only about a third of the colony's men were considered worthy to vote for the highest officials. These men were called "**freemen**." Deputies, or representatives, were to be elected by all male inhabitants, regardless of whether they had been approved for full church membership. However, **Quakers**, **atheists**, and Jews were forbidden to take part in elections.

The deputies—similar to the elected assemblymen in

> FREEMAN: FREE, WHITE, LANDOWNING MAN, OVER 21 YEARS OLD, WHO HAD THE RIGHT TO VOTE OR HOLD OFFICE
>
> QUAKER: ORIGINALLY A TERM OF MOCKERY GIVEN TO MEMBERS OF THE SOCIETY OF FRIENDS, A CHRISTIAN GROUP FOUNDED IN ENGLAND AROUND 1650
>
> ATHEIST: ONE WHO BELIEVES THAT THERE IS NO GOD

In New England, each town was governed by select citizens at town meetings. The right to vote on town decisions was limited to so-called "freemen" who had been approved by Puritan authorities.

Connecticut

other colonies—were to meet separately from the governor and magistrates. The deputies also had the sole authority to call the General Court—the name for Connecticut's lawmaking body—into session. This prevented the advisers from dominating the colony as they did in Massachusetts. The Fundamental Orders, however, left no doubt that the main purpose of the government was to preserve the Puritans' religion. Connecticut authorities arrested and banished non-Puritans.

Reverend John Davenport and the Puritan London merchant Theophilus Eaton had founded New Haven in 1637. Most New Haven settlers were Puritans from London. Davenport bought coastal land from the Native Americans because the merchants in his congregation wanted a seaport. New Haven set up a government similar to that of Massachusetts, where church members held all the power. The New Haven government remained separate from the rest of Connecticut. Eaton ruled as governor for 20 years, faithfully following the advice of the clergy.

Even the work of building a new settlement in the wilderness stopped on Sunday. The lack of a church did not keep the Puritans of New Haven from their Sunday worship.

The English Tide

A New Charter

In 1649, the English Civil War ended in the execution of King Charles I. Connecticut and Massachusetts especially welcomed the rule of Oliver Cromwell, a Puritan. Cromwell ruled **Parliament,** and through it, England. After Cromwell's death, England's Puritan Commonwealth came to an end in 1660. The monarchy was restored when Charles II, son of Charles I, was named king. The American colonies each had to decide whether they should declare their loyalty to the king, or whether they should wait to see if he was driven back into exile. Finally, when it looked like Charles II was on the throne to stay, Connecticut declared loyalty to the throne in 1661. New Haven followed a few months later.

In 1662 Connecticut sent John Winthrop Jr. to England to request confirmation of the colony's charter. Charles II granted a charter to Connecticut that closely resembled the original Fundamental Orders. The new charter also combined Connecticut and New Haven into one colony. New Haven objected to losing its independence and accused Winthrop of double-dealing. The king may have been punishing New Haven because two men involved in the killing of his father, Charles I, were known to be hiding there.

Above: Oliver Cromwell ruled England after the execution of King Charles I. When Cromwell died in 1658, his son could not hold onto power. Charles II returned to rule England in 1660.

Left: King Charles I was charged with treason before he was executed. William Goffe and Edward Whalley, two of the judges who had sentenced the king (shown here hiding from pursuers) to death, fled England and took refuge in New Haven when King Charles II was restored to the throne. The Puritans of New Haven refused to turn the fugitives over to royal authorities. New Haven's three-month delay in recognizing Charles II may also have cost the small colony independence from the rest of Connecticut.

Connecticut

4. Making a Living in Connecticut

English people from Massachusetts and England continued to flock to Connecticut, drawn by the promise of good farm land. Each settlement started with the building of a town, with individual house lots arranged around the town common. A church, school, and home for the minister stood in the center of town. Fields for farming surrounded the town, and inhabitants were granted the right to use the fields. Puritans expected their people to live close together in town so the

Making a Living in Connecticut

WEST INDIES: ISLANDS OF THE CARIBBEAN SEA, SO CALLED BECAUSE THE FIRST EUROPEAN VISITORS THOUGHT THEY WERE NEAR INDIA

authorities and neighbors could keep an eye on their behavior. However, farmers found it inconvenient to travel to their fields, so they began moving out of the towns to live on their land, and so became more independent.

More than 90% of the population worked at farming. First, farmers sought to support themselves and their families. Then they worked to produce surplus crops and animals for sale, so they could make enough money to buy tools and other goods that they couldn't produce on their own. Early crops included corn, wheat, rye, peas, flax, and tobacco. Few people or businesses used actual money, but instead bargained their goods and labor.

Connecticut exported tobacco and flour as well as salted or pickled beef and pork. The meat was shipped to the **West Indies** and Europe. In exchange for meat, the West Indies sent back sugar and molasses. Molasses was made into rum at distilleries in New England.

A view of Middletown, which grew to be a busy port in the 1700s

Connecticut

Making a Living in Connecticut

Several ports and shipbuilding centers—including New London, Saybrook, and Norwich—had been built along Connecticut's long coastline beginning in the mid-1600s. But no single port conducted significant foreign trade. Connecticut farmers exported their surplus grain, livestock, and meat from the major ports of Boston or New York instead of from their own coastal towns. **Peddlers** bought household goods in port towns and carted them through the countryside, selling the goods from door to door. By the mid-1700s, such businesses as iron forges, tinsmiths, clock makers, and gunsmiths became common in Connecticut.

Left: Connecticut's population of farmers spread out from the towns in order to live on their farmland.

Below: The rocky soil of New England—"before" and "after."

Connecticut

Above: The Yankee peddler's cart became a familiar sight on Connecticut's country roads.

As in the rest of New England, people turned from farming to other occupations. The forests, rivers, and ocean provided ways to make a living. Lumber and wood products became a major export. People built grist mills along the rivers to grind wheat into flour. On the coast, men found work fishing, whaling, and building ships.

Metal dishes, pots, and pans were among the items sold by peddlers.

Making a Living in Connecticut

The Uses of the Whale

In the early days of English settlement in Connecticut, whalers had to go no farther than the Long Island Sound, which was just offshore. Both colonists and Native Americans sent out small boats from the Connecticut shore to hunt and kill whales. After a century of English settlement, whales became harder to find near shore, and whalers sailed out from New England ports to hunt whales in the North Atlantic. Eventually, after the end of America's colonial period, whalers sailed all the oceans of the world in search of whales.

Whale oil taken from the carcasses was used to make candles and lamp oil. People of many nations depended on whale oil for light until petroleum came into use in the 1800s. So-called whalebone, actually a flexible material from the mouth of a certain type of whale, became a popular material from which to make combs and other items. Ambergris, found in sperm whale intestines, became an important ingredient of perfume.

Catching whales was dangerous work. Whaling grew more important in the 1800s, and many whaling ships operated out of Mystic seaport.

5. New England Battles

King Philip's War

As more and more English colonists settled New England, Native Americans saw that their way of life was in peril. White settlements surrounded many native villages. English livestock trampled and ate their corn crops. As the colonists cleared woodlands to create farms, animals for hunting retreated inland, and Native American hunters had to travel farther and farther to have successful hunts.

The Wampanoags had lived in peace with the English ever since 1620 when their leader, Massasoit, made a treaty of friendship with the Pilgrims. Massasoit's son, Metacom, called King Philip by the English, saw that he was losing control of his lands and his power. As the English forced him to give up more and more land, Metacom organized a confederacy to resist English expansion.

An artist's idea of Metacom, or King Philip, meeting with the English authorities. Metacom is shown dressed as a Native American from the Great Plains, a part of America not yet seen by the English.

New England Battles

The New England colonies joined together to fight King Philip. By the fall of 1675, the Narragansetts, Pocumtucs, and Nipmucs joined the Wampanoags in the battle against the English. The Mohegans and the few remaining Pequots joined with the English. At first the enemy Native Americans enjoyed great success and destroyed several colonial villages. The enemy made it impossible for the **frontier** villages to communicate with one another. Knowing that they were vulnerable to attack, many settlers abandoned their homes and fled eastward for safety.

Connecticut sent about 300 English and 150 Native American fighting men up the Connecticut River valley into western Massachusetts to help fight the enemy. However, Connecticut was concerned about defending its own people as well, and Connecticut and Massachusetts officers quarreled over where to send the troops.

In December 1675, the governor of Plymouth, Josiah Winslow, and Robert Treat of Connecticut led their combined forces in an attack against Metacom's most

The Mohegan sachem, Uncas, meeting with the English. In 1637, Uncas had commanded a force of Mohegans and helped the English massacre a Pequot village. The following year, he told Governor John Winthrop, "This heart is not mine, but yours; I have no men; they are all yours; command me any difficult thing, I will do it." His people fought on the English side again in 1675. Under the leadership of Uncas, the Mohegans remained allies of the English for more than 40 years. Uncas lived until 1683.

Connecticut

ALLIES: PEOPLE OR NATIONS WHO HAVE AGREED TO COOPERATE, OR TO FIGHT ON THE SAME SIDE IN A WAR

powerful **allies**, the Narragansetts. Winslow found the Narragansetts camped on high ground in the middle of a vast Rhode Island swamp. A bloody, day-long battle took place. The English lost 240 men killed and wounded, an enormous number for a battle in this era. But the Narragansetts suffered more than 900 people killed and wounded.

During the winter of 1675–1676, the surviving Native Americans continued to raid throughout New England. When spring came, most Native American fighting men had to concentrate on hunting and fishing in order to feed their families. The English had greater resources to support a war and so they kept hunting down the enemy.

The Great Swamp Fight of December 1675

Connecticut soldiers and their native allies conducted raids into enemy territory and killed another 200. By June, Massachusetts leaders offered to spare any Native American who surrendered. Hundreds took advantage of this offer. However, the Native Americans had killed one out of every 16 English fighting men. Although Massachusetts sold its captives into slavery, Connecticut limited its vengeance to ten years of servitude. Unlike the other New England colonies, Connecticut had not had any towns destroyed during the war.

All that remained was to track down Metacom himself. On August 12, 1676, a group of whites and their native allies found and killed him. Although some fighting continued for another two years, Metacom's death marked the end of the greatest—but not the last—military challenge the Native Americans ever mounted against colonists in New England.

By the end of King Philip's War in 1676, the Mohegans were the only important tribe still living in southern New England. However, relentless pressure from white settlement reduced both the Mohegans' territory and their population until they numbered 750 in 1705, and a mere 206 in 1774.

THE DOMINION OF NEW ENGLAND

At the start of King Philip's War, Sir Edmund Andros, royal governor of New York, had claimed that New York rightfully included western Connecticut all the way to the Connecticut River. Knowing that Connecticut was facing war, he had taken the opportunity to send two shiploads of soldiers to the Connecticut coast. Finding the fort at Saybrook fully manned, he retreated, but Connecticut had not seen the last of him.

After King Charles' death in 1685, his brother and successor, King James II, merged all the New England colonies, plus New York and New Jersey, into the Dominion of New England with Sir Edmund Andros as the royal governor. Massachusetts in particular had defied English laws, and the king wanted to bring Massachusetts back under his control.

First, the crown brought the colonies of Massachusetts Bay (which included Maine, Plymouth, and New Hampshire) under the Dominion. Rhode Island and Connecticut were the next to be taken over, followed by New Jersey and New York. Andros ordered Connecticut to turn over its charter to him in 1687. According to legend, Captain Joseph Wadsworth was said to have hidden the charter in a hollow oak tree in Hartford. The tree came to be called the "Charter Oak," although the legendary event may not have actually occurred. However,

Connecticut

Main picture: The Charter Oak is long gone, but a monument marks where it stood until 1856.

Below: Fact or fiction? Colonists hide the Charter in 1687.

with or without the actual charter in hand, Andros was in fact governor of Connecticut.

After James II was forced from the throne and William of Orange became king, the unwilling members of the Dominion took action to restore their independence. In 1689, Massachusetts captured and imprisoned Governor Andros. The other colonies then resumed governing themselves as they had before the creation of the Dominion. In time, King William officially restored Connecticut's charter as a separate royal colony, but not before he called upon the colonies to assist England in a war against the French.

KING WILLIAM'S WAR AND QUEEN ANNE'S WAR

England and France were great rivals who, throughout their history, had often resorted to war to resolve disagreements. Even during peaceful times they competed fiercely. When **British** and French settlers came to North

New England Battles

America, they brought their conflict with them. New France lay to the north of New England, in present-day Canada. However, Native American country lay between the English and French colonies, and many native peoples had become allies of the French. As the 1600s drew to a close, the French in North America and their Native American allies grew in numbers and strength, and frontier New Englanders lived in fear of attack. As Puritans and Protestants, they worried that Catholic missionaries from France would convert the native peoples and stir them up to fight a religious war.

Meanwhile, in 1688 England and France went to war with each other in Europe. The war continued until 1697. This war, known as King William's War, and another war that raged from 1701 to 1714, spilled over into the American colonies. Throughout those years, French and Native American forces attacked New England settlements, and New England forces and their Native American allies attacked French settlements in a never-ending cycle of attacks and revenge. Connecticut towns, however, did not suffer any attacks.

English colonists in New England and New York planned an invasion of Canada but were never able to assemble enough troops to do so. In addition to patrolling its own borders, Connecticut contributed more than 100 militiamen and a large amount of money to the defense of Albany, New York, and Massachusetts towns in the Connecticut River Valley

The war known as Queen Anne's War broke out in 1701, but Connecticut did not participate until it came to the assistance of Massachusetts in 1704, when Deerfield fell to a Native American massacre. Connecticut also agreed to join the neighboring colonies and the British navy in an invasion

King William III and Queen Mary II. William was both the nephew of James II and his son-in-law. William lived in the Netherlands with his wife Mary, the daughter of James II. James II was Catholic, and William and Mary were Protestants. Discontented Protestants in England wrote to William inviting him to England. William landed in England with an army, and James fled to France.

39

of Montreal in 1709, but the invasion was called off when the fleet failed to arrive. Connecticut sent 300 men to participate in the capture of Port Royal, Nova Scotia, the following year.

When Queen Anne's War ended in Europe in 1714, the French gave up their possessions of Newfoundland and Nova Scotia to the British. However, France still held a part of Canada bordering New England. Both New York and Massachusetts expected Connecticut to continue supplying troops to their militias to help them patrol the border during peacetime, but Connecticut refused.

Fifteen years after the end of Queen Anne's War, another war with France appeared likely. Connecticut began buying cannons, building a warship, and erecting forts along its

A World at War

During the colonial period in North America, war between England and other European powers was a regular occurrence. Between 1652 and 1674, England fought three wars with the Netherlands. Then in 1688, England began the first of four wars against France. During each of these wars, battles took place in Europe, at sea, and in the American colonies held by each of the warring European powers.

From 1688 to 1697, England and the Netherlands, formerly enemies, joined together to fight against France. This war was called the War of the Grand Alliance or the Nine Years' War in Europe. In America it was called King William's War, and battles took place in New York, New England, and Canada.

From 1701 to 1714, England fought France and Spain in the War of the Spanish Succession. In America, the war was called Queen Anne's War, and fighting took place in Canada, New England, South Carolina, and Florida.

From 1740 to 1748, Great Britain fought Spain, France and other European powers in the War of the Austrian Succession. The war had begun in Europe in 1740, but France did not enter the war until 1744, when it declared war on Britain and attacked the British-held town of Annapolis Royal, Nova Scotia. In America, the war was called King George's War, and most of the battles took place in Nova Scotia. French and Native American raiders also attacked settlements in what is now Maine.

The so-called Seven Years' War between France and Great Britain took place between 1754 and 1763. In America it was called the French and Indian War. Battles took place from Pennsylvania to Canada. Many American soldiers learned about war during the French and Indian War. They used this experience when they fought the British in the Revolutionary War.

frontiers. The colony also sent several hundred militiamen to New York and Massachusetts. When King George's War broke out in 1744, 500 Connecticut militia joined with the rest of New England and captured the French fortress at Louisbourg, on Cape Breton Island at the eastern end of Nova Scotia, in 1745. Louisbourg, however became a bargaining chip in peace negotiations and was returned to France at the end of King George's War in 1748. Only six more years would pass before France and **Great Britain** went to war for the fourth time.

Religious Revival

As war raged in the neighboring colonies, Connecticut settlers continued to spread out along the coast and river

> GREAT BRITAIN: NATION FORMED BY ENGLAND, WALES, SCOTLAND, AND NORTHERN IRELAND; "GREAT BRITAIN" CAME INTO USE WHEN ENGLAND AND SCOTLAND FORMALLY UNIFIED IN 1707

New England troops invade Canada and capture Louisbourg.

Connecticut

Below: The town of New London. The people of the newer towns were not as religious as those of the original towns and did not welcome interference from the Puritan government of Connecticut.

New England Battles

Right: George Whitefield spent more than a year preaching in the colonies, traveling from Georgia to Maine.

valleys, forming at least 70 towns by the Revolution. They had their Puritan religious beliefs in common, but each community pursued its separate path. Connecticut made the Puritans' Congregational church the established religion. Local Congregational churches were supported by public funds. However, in 1708, Connecticut allowed Baptists to practice their religion. The first Anglican church did not begin operating in Connecticut until 1722. Even so, non-Puritans still had to pay to support Congregational churches.

While many New Englanders devoted themselves to making money, others believed that the Puritans were straying too far from their religious roots. This belief led to the revival of religious spirit, a movement called the Great Awakening. It started in Massachusetts where a brilliant religious thinker, Jonathan Edwards, preached about the need for people to rely on God's power to redeem themselves. The powerful message spread across the colonies.

Thousands of people gathered to hear the preaching of George Whitefield, one of the founders of the **Methodist Church in Great Britain**. Methodists were former Anglicans who, like the Puritans before them, found the

43

Connecticut

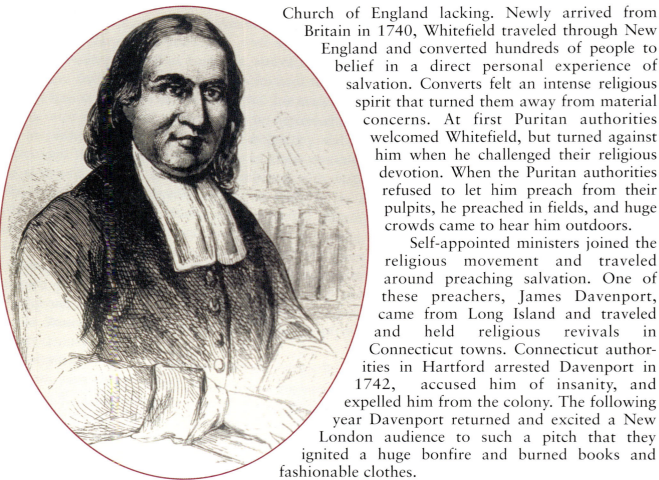

Samson Occom became a preacher after attending a Christian charity school in Lebanon, Connecticut.

> **EVANGELIST:** TRAVELING PREACHER WHO SEEKS TO WIN CONVERTS TO A RELIGION BY PREACHING AT REVIVAL MEETINGS

Church of England lacking. Newly arrived from Britain in 1740, Whitefield traveled through New England and converted hundreds of people to belief in a direct personal experience of salvation. Converts felt an intense religious spirit that turned them away from material concerns. At first Puritan authorities welcomed Whitefield, but turned against him when he challenged their religious devotion. When the Puritan authorities refused to let him preach from their pulpits, he preached in fields, and huge crowds came to hear him outdoors.

Self-appointed ministers joined the religious movement and traveled around preaching salvation. One of these preachers, James Davenport, came from Long Island and traveled and held religious revivals in Connecticut towns. Connecticut authorities in Hartford arrested Davenport in 1742, accused him of insanity, and expelled him from the colony. The following year Davenport returned and excited a New London audience to such a pitch that they ignited a huge bonfire and burned books and fashionable clothes.

The emotional evangelical style of preaching attracted some Pequots and Mohegans to Christianity. One Mohegan, Samson Occom, had converted to Christianity at the age of 16 after hearing James Davenport preach. He attended a school for native peoples founded by **evangelists**, and then worked as a missionary among Montauks of Long Island. A good student and gifted speaker, Occom was sent to England to preach in 1766 and raised about ten thousand pounds, an enormous amount of money for the time. His speaking skill and religious devotion drew crowds of English people who were curious to see the rarity of a Native American preacher. However, on Occom's return to Connecticut, he was ignored and the money he raised was used to build a new college in New Hampshire, Dartmouth, that educated primarily white people.

6.
THE ROAD TO INDEPENDENCE

THE FRENCH AND INDIAN WAR

Despite the defeats France had suffered at the hands of the British in the first half of the 18th century, French explorers claimed all of North America from the Allegheny Mountains to the Rocky Mountains and from Canada to Mexico. Few French people settled in this vast area south of Canada. Instead, French traders followed the waterways to hunt and trap and to trade with the Native Americans. In the meantime British traders traveled westward to the far side of the Allegheny Mountains, to trade with the native peoples of the Ohio River valley. France wanted to keep control of the Ohio Valley, but British colonists wanted to expand westward.

As this 1755 map shows, the British believed that their colonies extended across the continent. Connecticut authorities argued that their territory cut across New York and Pennsylvania to extend to the west. Accordingly, after the French and Indian War, a group of settlers from Connecticut moved to the Wyoming Valley of Pennsylvania and organized it as a county of Connecticut. Pennsylvania and Connecticut argued over the land until 1782, when the Continental government awarded the disputed territory to Pennsylvania.

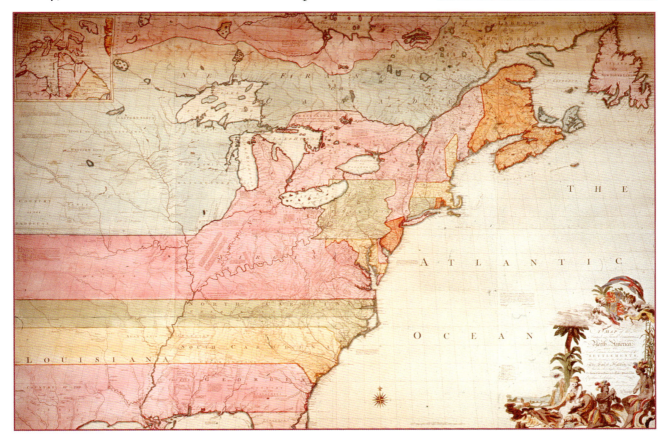

Connecticut

Concerned about French maneuvers in the west, representatives from the New England colonies, Pennsylvania, Maryland, and the Iroquois peoples of New York met in Albany in June 1754 to discuss cooperation against the French. The Albany Congress also discussed a bold plan for a union among the colonies, but in the end, the colonies feared that they would lose control over their own affairs. Connecticut representatives argued that they had already contributed enough money and manpower to fighting the French, even though the French had not directly endangered Connecticut.

A month later, a new war between the French and the British began on disputed land near modern-day Pittsburgh, Pennsylvania, with a small battle between Virginia militia and French soldiers. This battle to control

George Washington was a young officer of the Virginia militia when he led his men into the first battle of the French and Indian War.

The Road to Independence

the Ohio River valley erupted into a long and deadly conflict. In Europe the war became known as the Seven Years' War. Americans called it the French and Indian War.

In the end, Connecticut agreed to contribute to the war effort, sending 1,500 men to help build forts on the Hudson River. Over the course of the war, Connecticut sent thousands more troops to the Hudson River valley in response to British calls for assistance. Although none of the battles took place on Connecticut soil, leading Connecticut colonists had a good life under British rule and did not want to anger the king by refusing to cooperate.

REVOLUTION

After France and Great Britain made peace in 1763, British leaders concluded that the American colonies had

The Battle of Lake George in New York. Nearly half of all New England men aged 16 to 29 served in the French and Indian War.

Connecticut

not contributed as much to the war as they should have. Moreover, the British government still needed to provide soldiers to defend the colonies from possible future attacks. This was a heavy expense. Never before had the British Parliament set taxes on American colonists. This changed in 1764. To help pay for the cost of defending the colonies, Parliament passed the Sugar Act to raise money from the American colonies themselves.

The Sugar Act imposed taxes on imports and exports. Such taxes are called duties. The Sugar Act placed duties on refined sugar as well as other trade goods and provided for strict enforcement and collection procedures. The law taxed Connecticut's trade at a time when the colony was struggling to recover from spending so much money on outfitting the war. It was the first in a series of decisions made by the British Parliament that eventually led to the American Revolution.

Next, in 1765 Parliament passed the Stamp Act. Under the Stamp Act, colonists had to pay to have most documents stamped, or risk arrest. Even newspapers had

Colonists met to discuss ways to resist the Stamp Act.

The Road to Independence

to have stamps. The Stamp Act affected colonists of all social classes, and resistance grew throughout the colonies. Although riots broke out in many colonies, and groups calling themselves the Sons of Liberty attacked the offices and homes of tax collectors, Connecticut protesters remained orderly and nonviolent as they forced Connecticut's stamp agent to resign.

Connecticut's Sons of Liberty, however, swore that they were prepared to fight for the right of the colonies to make their own decisions about taxes. They organized a convention and voted to eject Connecticut's royal governor, Thomas Fitch, and his supporters from office and replace them with men they would choose.

So unpopular was the Stamp Act that Parliament repealed it in 1766. Still, King George III insisted that Great Britain's Parliament had the right to make laws for the colonies and collect taxes. Britain passed a new set of laws taxing even more products, and angering more colonists. Tensions continued to grow between colonists and British soldiers and officials. Connecticut's assembly

A British cartoonist mocked the repeal of the Stamp Act with a picture of its "funeral."

49

Connecticut

The destruction of a tea shipment in Boston Harbor, known to history as the Boston Tea Party

The Road to Independence

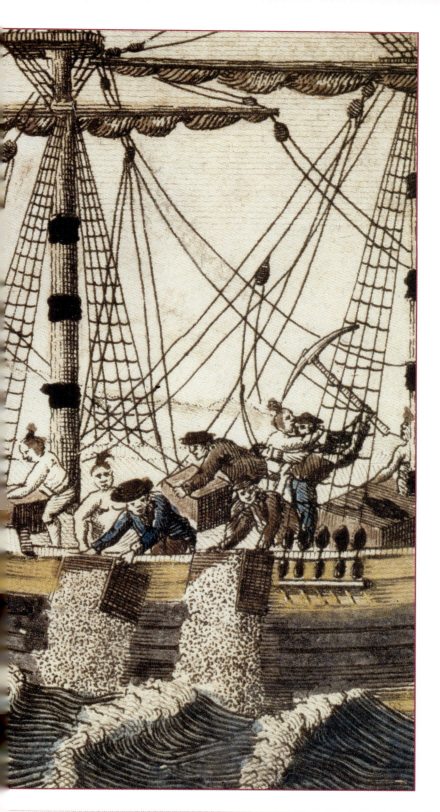

sent a letter of protest to the king, and its merchants resorted to **smuggling** to evade taxes.

Colonial leaders protested what they considered unjust British rule, but they were against violence. Among the peaceful ways protesters opposed British laws was through the formation of Committees of Correspondence. By writing letters, the Committees kept one another informed and made plans for the colonies to cooperate. The Committees convinced all the colonies except New Hampshire to **boycott** English merchandise. In Connecticut, people found to be trading with Britain risked having their names published in the newspapers. The boycott convinced the British to repeal most taxes by 1770.

Then Parliament passed a law that gave one British tea seller, the East India Company, special treatment. The East India Company was given a monopoly in the colonies so that it could sell its tea more cheaply than any other dealer. Once again, the Committees of Correspondence went to work, spreading news of the new law and the coming East India Company tea shipments. The Sons of Liberty organized actions against the shipments. The first such action, the famous Boston Tea Party, occurred in December 1773 with the dumping of a large tea shipment into Boston Harbor. Britain responded by closing the port of Boston and placing Massachusetts under military rule. Connecticut **patriots** sent food and herded livestock to help feed the people of Boston.

Connecticut

A veteran of the French and Indian War, the popular Israel Putnam was a devoted patriot. He was appointed second in command of the Connecticut force sent to Massachusetts and—despite his age, nearly 60—became a general in the Continental Army. Many legends grew up about him, and one of them is portrayed in this painting in the U. S. Capitol. He was said to have left his plow and ridden one of his plow horses to battle when he heard about the fighting at Lexington

People throughout the colonies began to argue that they would have to fight for their rights. All of the colonies except Georgia agreed to send delegates to the First Continental Congress in Philadelphia, to be held in September 1774.

The Congress drew up a set of resolutions stating the rights of the colonies to self-government and formed a Continental Association to boycott English trade goods and organize local governments. The delegates agreed to meet again in May 1775. Before that date arrived, the first battle of the American Revolution had been fought on April 19 in Lexington, Massachusetts.

Seeing its neighbor in peril, Connecticut abandoned its peaceful protests, as men picked up their muskets and headed to Massachusetts. About 3,000 men from Connecticut marched to Massachusetts to help fight the British. The governor, Jonathan Trumbull, had helped found the local Sons of Liberty and supported the Revolution. He wrote to the British general in Boston that "outrages have been committed as would disgrace even barbarians." Connecticut set about buying ships to form a

The Road to Independence

navy and building defenses along its coast. The government even freed some prisoners so they could join the militia. Only a small portion of the population, about 5 or 6 percent, remained loyal to Great Britain.

Throughout the war, Connecticut provided weapons and food for the Continental army. The iron works at Salisbury produced guns, cannons, and cannonballs. The Simsbury copper mine, which had begun operating near Hartford in 1709, was converted into a prison in 1773 and renamed Newgate, after an infamous prison in Great Britain. During the war, the prison held some **loyalists** as well as deserters from the Continental Army.

Below: Governor Jonathan Trumbull supervises the loading of supplies for the Continental army. Despite his efforts, the army was not well supplied. A Connecticut soldier wrote to the governor from a fort in New York, complaining, "The men at this place, belonging to the colony of Connecticut, think they are not well used, as they were promised several things, they don't think there are any steps taken to fulfil it … . Several of the companies have no brass kettles to this day. I got one for my company … . Several companies have no frying pans … . Our water here is very bad and unwholesome. … I think there has not been one pound of soap brought for the Army … ."

Nathan Hale and Benedict Arnold

As the colonies broke out into open rebellion against British rule, two Connecticut men quickly offered their service to the Revolutionary cause: Nathan Hale and Benedict Arnold.

Born in 1755, Nathan Hale was one of nine sons of a prosperous farmer. He graduated from Yale and became a schoolteacher. In July 1775, he joined the rebel Connecticut militia, and a few months later became a captain in the Continental Army. While serving in New York, Hale volunteered when George Washington asked for a man to carry out a special mission behind enemy lines. He spent several days gathering information about British troop positions on Long Island. Hale proved to be a true patriot but a bungling spy. On his return journey, he was captured by the British. The papers he carried proved he was a spy. Since he was out of uniform, he was found guilty of spying and sentenced to hang. Before his execution the next morning, September 22, 1776, the 21-year-old said, "I only regret that I have but one life to lose for my country."

As Connecticut men rushed off to help Massachusetts in the wake of the battle of Lexington and Concord, Benedict Arnold of New Haven

The East Haddam, Connecticut, schoolhouse where Nathan Hale taught

The execution of Nathan Hale

The Road to Independence

was among the first. So determined was he to supply the rebels that he threatened to use force to get gunpowder from his town's storehouse.

Born in 1741 in Norwich, he was actually Benedict Arnold V. The first Benedict Arnold had been governor of the colony of Rhode Island in the 1650s. Benedict had been one of six children, but only he and a sister survived to adulthood. After the others died during an epidemic, Benedict's father took to drinking and lost the successful family business. Benedict was forced to leave school, which his family could no longer afford, at the age of 15, and become an apprentice to a druggist. Arnold worked hard to restore his family's fortunes and became successful enough to open his own shop at the age of 21. He went on to become a wealthy merchant and the owner of several trading ships. He married in 1767, and he and his wife had three sons.

Benedict Arnold left a thriving business, growing family, and fine home to organize a company of militia and join the revolution. His wife died while he was at war. He was a brave and talented military leader and became a major general in the Continental Army. His leadership during the Saratoga campaign greatly helped the rebels defeat the British. After receiving a serious wound, Arnold became military governor of Philadelphia in 1778. There he remarried and fell under suspicion for mismanaging public money.

Few remember that Benedict Arnold and his men endured great hardship for the American cause when they marched through Maine to Quebec in November 1775.

In 1779, Arnold began secretly helping the British and selling them valuable information about American troop movements. When he was assigned to the command of West Point, he made plans to leave it nearly unguarded so the British could easily capture it. The next year American forces discovered his plan, and Arnold fled to a British warship. Later in the war, he became a general in the British army and led raids against American positions.

After the Revolution, Benedict Arnold returned to trading in Canada and London, accompanied by his second wife and their four sons, his sister, and his three sons from his first marriage. He was widely mistrusted and fell into poverty. He died a poor man in London in 1801. Several of his sons and grandsons became officers in the British army. Arnold's early contributions to the American cause are forgotten. Instead, he is remembered for being a traitor.

Connecticut

No major battles took place in Connecticut, although the British raided a number of coastal towns. Several Connecticut men played notable roles in the war, including Israel Putnam, Nathan Hale, and Benedict Arnold. Benedict Arnold was a valiant American officer who went over to the British side. Arnold led a British raid against his home state at New London in 1781. His soldiers destroyed numerous ships and much of the town.

Governor Trumbull's son John became an artist and painted many scenes from the American Revolution, including this one. Three Connecticut men, Silas Deane, Eliphalet Dyer, and Roger Sherman attended the First Continental Congress. The Declaration of Independence was signed at the Second Continental Congress by four Connecticut men, Samuel Huntington, Roger Sherman, William Williams, and Oliver Wolcott.

Epilogue

After the Revolution, Connecticut became the fifth state to approve the United States Constitution, on January 9, 1788. Hartford is the state capital, and Bridgeport is the largest city. Other major cities include New Haven, Waterbury, and Stamford. New Haven is the home of Yale University, one of the nation's most famous universities, founded in 1701.

About 3.5 million people live in Connecticut. Approximately 9 percent of the population is black, and another 9 percent are either Asian, Hispanic, or Native American. About 4,000 people are of Native American ancestry. The white population was once mostly British but now includes Italian-Americans and descendants of Polish, Irish, and French Canadian immigrants.

As farm land grew scarce and less fertile, many people gave up farming and went to work in factories during the 1800s. Today, one percent of Connecticut's workers are in agriculture and twenty-five percent in manufacturing.

A Wethersfield, Connecticut, house built around 1720 and still open to visitors

Connecticut

Farm products include apples, corn, potatoes, tomatoes, livestock, eggs, milk, and flowers and shrubs. However, the state's tobacco crops earn the most money.

Connecticut's factories produce tools, machinery, electronic goods, jet engines, submarines, chemicals, and plastic products, as well as firearms and clocks. Clocks have been made in Connecticut since colonial times, and the Colt six-shooter was developed in Connecticut in 1835.

Another important Connecticut industry is insurance, with at least 100 companies, mostly in Hartford. The industry began with early merchants' need to insure their shipments at sea.

Connecticut has just one commercial fishing fleet, operating out of Stonington, but aquaculture—growing

Yale College during colonial times

Epilogue

seafood in underwater "farms"—thrives in Connecticut. Connecticut is a major producer of farm-raised oysters as well as other seafood.

Visitors interested in Connecticut's early history can visit Old Newgate Prison and Copper Mine at East Granby, near Hartford, and the Pequot Museum at Ledyard in the southeastern part of the state. Several restored colonial buildings can be visited in Wethersfield.

Center Church in Hartford's historic center stands in front of the Travelers Tower, a famous city landmark. Hartford's founder, Thomas Hooker, is believed to lie buried near a corner of the church.

Connecticut

DATELINE

1524: Giovanni da Verrazano explores the coast of New England.

1603: Martin Pring leads a trading expedition to New England in search of sassafras and other goods.

1614: Dutch explorer Adriaen Block explores about 50 miles of the Connecticut River. Captain John Smith explores and maps the New England coast. His book about his voyage promotes interest in the area as a potential colony.

1631: Dutch traders from New Netherland build a trading post, Fort Good Hope, near present-day Hartford.

1632: Edward Winslow of Plymouth Colony explores the Connecticut River valley.

1633: A group of settlers from Plymouth buys riverside land from the Native Americans and builds a settlement that later becomes part of Windsor, Connecticut.

1636: Thomas Hooker leads his congregation from Massachusetts to build a new settlement at Hartford, Connecticut.

1637: New England colonists slaughter hundreds of Pequots and take over their land. The town of New Haven is established as a colony independent of the rest of Connecticut.

1639: Men from the towns of Hartford, Windsor, and Wethersfield draw up a governing document for Connecticut called the Fundamental Orders.

1662: Connecticut—now including New Haven—receives a charter from King Charles II of England.

1675–1676: King Philip's War, between the New England colonists and the Wampanoags and other Native Americans, results in defeat of the Wampanoags and the death of their chief, Metacom, or King Philip.

1687: King James II forces Connecticut to join the Dominion of New England, governed by Sir Edmund Andros. Andros demands that Connecticut hand over its charter, but legend claims the document is hidden in a hollow tree.

1765: In protest of British taxes, Connecticut's Sons of Liberty organize a revolutionary government.

1781: Benedict Arnold, having turned traitor, leads a British attack on his home state and burns New London, Connecticut.

JANUARY 9, 1788: Connecticut becomes the fifth state to approve the United States Constitution.

GLOSSARY

ALGONQUIAN: Native American who speaks one of several related languages belonging to the Algonquian family of languages; Algonquian speakers once lived over an area extending from New England to the Carolinas, as well as in parts of Canada and around the Great Lakes

ALLIES: people or nations who have agreed to cooperate, or to fight on the same side in a war

AMERICA: land that contains the continents of North America and South America

ANGLICAN: Church of England, a Protestant church and the state church of England

ATHEIST: one who believes that there is no God

BOYCOTT: agreement to refuse to buy from or sell to certain businesses

BRITISH: nationality of a person born in Great Britain; people born in England are called "English"

CHARTER: document containing the rules for running an organization

DUTCH: nationality of people born in the Netherlands

DUTY: tax collected on goods brought into a country

DYNASTY: series of rulers from the same family, who pass the throne from one family member to another

EVANGELIST: traveling preacher who seeks to win converts to a religion by preaching at revival meetings

FREEMAN: free, white, landowning man, over 21 years old, who had the right to vote or hold office

GREAT BRITAIN: nation formed by England, Wales, Scotland, and Northern Ireland; "Great Britain" came into use when England and Scotland formally unified in 1707

INDIAN: the name given to all Native Americans at the time Europeans first came to America, because it was believed that America was actually a close neighbor of India

LOYALIST: colonist who wanted America to remain a colony of Great Britain

METHODIST: member of a Protestant church founded by George Whitefield and others in England during the mid-1700s

MILITIA: group of citizens not normally part of the army who join together to defend their land in an emergency

NATIVE AMERICANS: people who had been living in America for thousands of years at the time that the first Europeans arrived

PARLIAMENT: legislature of Great Britain

PATRIOT: American who wanted the colonies to be independent of Great Britain

PEDDLER: one who travels around selling small items

PILGRIM: Puritan who separated from the Church of England instead of trying to change it from within

PROTESTANT: any Christian church that has broken from away from Roman Catholic or Eastern Orthodox control

PURITANS: Protestants who wanted the Church of England to practice a more "pure" form of Christianity

QUAKER: originally a term of mockery given to members of the Society of Friends, a Christian group founded in England around 1650

SACHEM: Algonquian word for chief

SASSAFRAS: type of tree whose bark is used for flavoring or medicinal purposes

SMUGGLING: secretly and illegally trading in forbidden merchandise, or hiding goods to avoid paying taxes on them

TRAITOR: someone who betrays his or her country; treason is the crime committed by a traitor

WEST INDIES: the islands of the Caribbean Sea, so called because the first European visitors thought they were near India

FURTHER READING

Brenner, Barbara. *If You Were There in 1776*. New York: Bradbury Press, 1994.

Gourley, Catherine. *Welcome to Felicity's World, 1774: Life in Colonial America*. Middleton, Wis.: Pleasant Company Publications, 1999.

Newman, Shirlee Petkin. *The Pequots*. Danbury, Conn.: Franklin Watts, 2000.

Smith, Carter, ed. *Daily Life: A Source Book on Colonial America*. Brookfield, Conn.: Millbrook Press, 1991.

Smith, Carter, ed. *Governing and Teaching: A Source Book on Colonial America.* Brookfield, Conn.: Millbrook Press, 1991.

Tunis, Edwin. *Colonial Living.* Baltimore: Johns Hopkins University Press, 1999.

Wilbur, C. Keith. *The New England Indians.* Chester, Conn.: Globe Pequot Press, 1990.

WEBSITES

http://www.americaslibrary.gov
Select "Jump back in time" for links to history activities

http://www.cthistoryonline.org
Take virtual tours based on historical pictures

http://www.hfmgv.org/education/smartfun/colonial/intro/index.html
Go on a visit to a colonial farm family in Connecticut

http://www.thinkquest.org/library/JR_index.html
Explore links to numerous student-designed sites about American colonial history

BIBLIOGRAPHY

Hawke, David Freeman. *Everyday Life in Early America.* New York: Harper & Row, 1988.

Middleton, Richard. *Colonial America: A History, 1607–1760.* Cambridge, Mass.: Blackwell, 1992.

Perry, Charles Edward. *Founders and Leaders of Connecticut, 1633–1783.* Boston: D.C. Heath, 1934.

Taylor, Alan. *American Colonies.* New York: Viking, 2001.

Taylor, Robert J. *Colonial Connecticut: A History.* Millwood, N.Y.: KTO Press, 1979.

The American Heritage History of the Thirteen Colonies. New York: American Heritage, 1967.

INDEX

Andros, Edmund 37-38
Arnold, Benedict 54-56
Block, Adriaen 11
Boston Tea Party 50-51

Canada 9, 39-41, 45, 55
Charles I 27
Charles II 27, 37
Charter Oak 37-38
climate 16
Columbus, Christopher 8
Continental Congress 52, 56
Cromwell, Oliver 27

Davenport, James 44
Davenport, John 26
Dominion of New England 37-38

Eaton, Theophilus 26
Edwards, Jonathan 43

Fort Good Hope 15
France 9-10, 38-41, 45-47
French and Indian War 46-47, 52

geography 16-17
government 19, 21-22, 25-27
Great Awakening 43-44

Hale, Nathan 54, 56
Hartford 15, 20-21, 44, 53, 57
Hooker, Thomas 20-21
Huntington, Samuel 56

Indians; see Native Americans

James II 37-39

King George's War 40-41

King Philip's War 34-37
King William's War 39-40

Mason, John 23
Massachusetts 6, 14-15, 19-21, 23, 25-27, 35-41, 43, 51-52
Massachusetts Bay Colony 14-15, 19, 37
Massasoit 34
Metacom 34-35, 37
Middletown 28-29
Native Americans 15-18, 22-24, 34-37, 39, 44, 57
  Algonquian 17-18
  Mahican 17
  Mohegan 17, 24, 35, 37, 44
  Montauk 44
  Narragansett 24, 35-36
  Niantic 17, 24
  Nipmuc 17, 35
  Pequot 17, 22-23, 35, 44, 59
  Pocumtuc 35
  Podunk 17
  Quinnipiac 17
  Wampanoag 34-35
  Wappinger 17
Netherlands 6-7, 11, 13-15
New England 10-11, 15, 17, 36-37, 39-41, 43, 47
New Haven 26-27, 57
New London 31, 42-44, 56
New Netherland 6, 15
New York 6, 15, 31, 37, 39-41, 46-47
Newgate 53, 59
Norwich 31

Occom, Samson 44
Oldham, John 20, 22

Pennsylvania 45-46
Pequot War 22-24
Pilgrims 13-14, 34

Plymouth 14-15, 19, 35, 37
population 17, 37, 57
Pring, Martin 10
Puritans 6, 13, 19, 24-28, 39, 42-44
Putnam, Israel 52, 56

Queen Anne's War 39-40

religion 11-14, 19, 39, 43-44
Revolutionary War 52-56
Rhode Island 36-37

Saybrook 23, 31, 37
Sherman, Roger 56
slaves 7, 24, 36
Smith, John 11
Stamp Act 48-49
Sugar Act 48

trade 15, 29, 31-33, 48
Treat, Robert 35
Trumbull, John 56
Trumbull, Jonathan 52-53

Uncas 35
Underhill, John 23-24

Verrazano, Giovanni da 9-10
Vespucci, Amerigo 8

Wadsworth, Joseph 37
Washington, George 46, 54
Wethersfield 20-21, 23, 57, 59
Whitefield, George 43-44
William and Mary 38-39
Williams, William 56
Windsor 11, 15, 20-21
Winslow, Edward 15
Winslow, Josiah 35-36
Winthrop, John 14, 19, 35
Winthrop, John, Jr. 25, 27
Wolcott, Oliver 56